The Children's Tree
of Terezin

Written by
Dede Harris

Illustrated by
Sara Akerlund

LEGACY

Written by Dede Harris

Cover illustration by Sara Akerlund

Jacket photographs by Christopher Hiltz

Additional art credits: **Sara Akerlund**: 1–32; **Christopher Hiltz**: 40–47; **Jewish Museum in Prague**: 38 (left); **Shutterstock.com**: 34 (top, bottom left, bottom right); **Yad Vashem**: 34 (bottom center, from Fotoarciv Pamatnitku Terezin), 36 (all, with bottom right from Broktowa Truda), 38 (right, from Rabi Chaim Seidler Feller, U.S.A.)

Published by:
Louis Weber, CEO
Publications International, Ltd.
8140 Lehigh Avenue
Morton Grove, IL 60053

ISBN: 978-1-68022-785-7

Manufactured in China.

8 7 6 5 4 3 2 1

Many will know this noble and poignant Holocaust story because of the cooperation of the:
Illinois Holocaust Museum and Education Center
and
Chicago Botanic Garden

I dedicate this book to:
Sam Harris, my husband and child survivor of the Holocaust
and
Irma Lauscher and the children of Theresienstadt
— Dede Harris

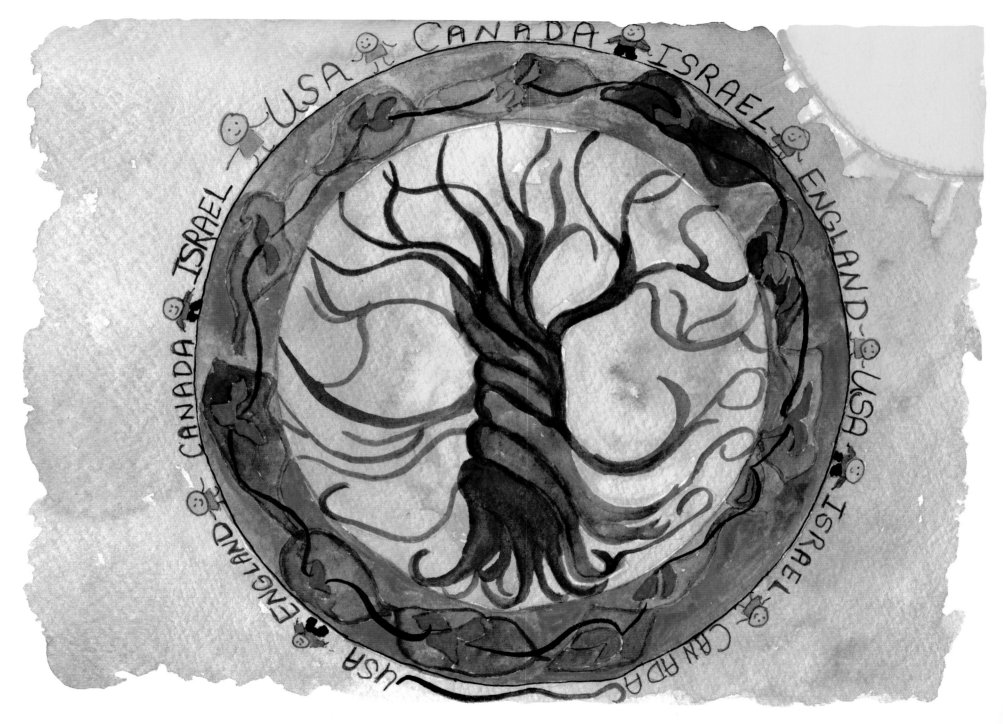

Sometimes you hear a story that makes you feel so much emotion that you want to honor it. The story of the Children's Tree of Terezin is one of those. It is a story of a remarkable and inspired woman, brave and caring children, and a little cutting of a silver maple tree. It is a story of kindness, generosity, and hope. It is a story that has spread throughout the world.

What is more, this story I am now going to tell you is true…

Between 1939 and 1945, the world was at war. Nazi dictator Adolf Hitler wanted Germany to take over the world. He invaded many countries.

Hitler hated the Jewish people and wanted to kill them. In Germany and the countries he conquered, he gathered the Jewish people, and any others he considered enemies, and put them in concentration camps. Large numbers of people were imprisoned in these concentration camps, usually without enough food, in crowded and dirty living conditions.

After the German army took over the country of Czechoslovakia, the Nazis set up Theresienstadt Concentration Camp, known by the Czechoslovakian people as Terezin. They imprisoned many Jewish people in this small area. Many of these people had been well-known before the War. They had distinguished themselves as authors, actors, musicians, and scientists.

Hitler used Terezin as a stage set because he wanted the world to see how well he treated his prisoners. But the stage set was a lie. Life in Terezin was terrible. Everyone was under constant threat of being moved from Terezin to an even more horrible place. The prisoners were crammed into small spaces. Starvation and disease were common. At first, there was no water system in Terezin, and a number of wells were contaminated. Typhoid fever broke out, and thousands died of disease and starvation.

Yet brave and inspiring things happened in Terezin.

The prisoners of Terezin believed that, despite their miserable conditions, the world was a place of beauty. Everyone could add to that beauty.

The adult prisoners established a Jewish Council in Terezin. This imprisoned council vowed that, despite everyone's persistent hunger, sickness, and fear, they would continue to support creative ideas and encourage each prisoner's imagination. The prisoners performed plays, operas, concerts, and musical productions. They wrote, drew, and painted. They found many ways to create beauty.

This council also decided that they would teach the children as much as they could.

Many prisoners taught the children. One teacher was Irma Lauscher. Irma's husband, Jiri, and their daughter, Michaela, were also prisoners in Terezin. They too were starving and afraid. Despite Irma's fears for herself and her family, she managed to think of others, especially the children in the camp. She was very concerned over the children's well being.

The young prisoners at the Terezin Concentration Camp attended secret classes. Teachers like Irma Lauscher encouraged them to continue to learn. Along with other lessons, she taught the children about the Jewish holidays.

The Jewish holiday of Tu B'Shevat was approaching. This holiday was always joyous, and a large part of it was the celebration of trees.

Irma wondered how she could celebrate this holiday that was meant to be full of hope and happiness with children who were suffering so enormously in this cruel concentration camp.

She found ways to emphasize hope. Although the prisoners did not have the traditional olives, dates, grapes, and figs to eat, the children drew pictures of the traditional foods. The prisoners thanked God for sustaining them and enabling them to reach the day of Tu B'Shevat.

And Irma had another idea.

To carry out her daring idea, Irma needed the help of a guard. While many of the Nazi and Czech guards were cruel, she knew a Czech guard who was kind. She asked him to bring the children a tree to plant.

Because it was illegal to bring anything in or out of the camp, the guard had to hide a small cutting from a tree. He put the cutting in his boot and smuggled it to Irma Lauscher and the children.

Irma organized a ceremony for the children for Tu B'Shevat. Behind one of the buildings where the children lived, they performed the ceremony and planted the tiny tree. They uttered speeches, quickly and quietly. They danced around the little cutting, singing "Am Yisrael Chai," which means "The Jewish People Live."

The ceremony meant so much to the people, and both old and young circled the tree.

A rabbi whispered a blessing to the children, saying, "Perhaps this tree will testify for us for years, perhaps for centuries. Perhaps this tree will be here and we will not. God grant that you may soon be planting trees in your own country, your own land, a land of freedom."

Water was rationed in the camp. Every day the children gave this little cutting a small amount of their rationed water and watched it grow.

Some children wrote poems about this sapling. They placed a sign at the foot of the sapling that read, "As the branches of this tree, so the branches of our people."

One child who was a prisoner in the camp wrote this poem:

"Here were three things the Nazis could not take from us.
They could not take the blue sky above us, for our gazing.
They could not take the flood of sunlight pouring into our courtyard, nourishing our tree and us.
But most of all, they could not take Our Invisible God who remained deep in our hearts."

As days and months passed, the children continued to water the tree. The tree's roots took hold and it became stronger and stronger.

Many of the prisoners in Terezin were sent to other concentration camps, where they were killed. But the tree in Terezin lived on, testifying to the memory of the children who had tended the tree, using their rationed water to ensure its growth. Eventually, the little cutting, planted and fed by the children of Terezin, grew into a beautiful silver maple tree.

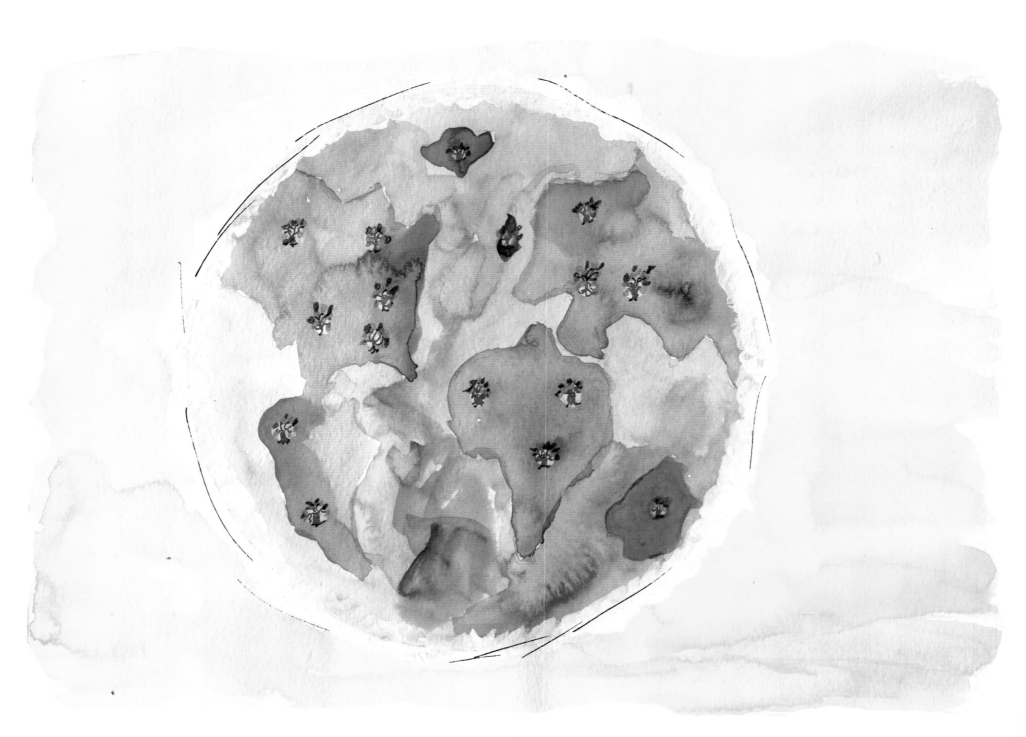

The tree was not forgotten after the war, and neither were the children of Terezin. Seeds and cuttings from the tree were sent around the world. From these seeds grew new trees that honor the memory of the children from Terezin and their story.

I will always remember this special woman, Irma Lauscher, who taught the children the selfless act of nursing the little cutting in spite of their own hunger and fear. The children learned many lessons from this simple act of planting and caring for a sapling. They learned to rise above the horrors around them to take care of a little living plant that needed their attention in order to thrive. They learned that even under terrible circumstances, one could always find a way to make life better. They learned that good people and good deeds do make a difference. The memory of Irma Lauscher and these brave children will live on for all who see the trees and read their story.

History

Nazi dictator Adolf Hitler took power in Germany in 1933. He wanted Germany to take over the world. The Nazis blamed Jews for Germany's economic problems, and laws were passed that restricted Jewish citizens' rights: Jews were not allowed to work in certain professions, serve in government, or attend public schools. German Jews were even prevented from using public transportation, sitting on park benches, and owning pets. The German government wanted Jews to leave the country. Many did, but many others who wanted to leave were unable to complete the necessary paperwork or gain entry visas from other countries.

With each year discrimination and violence against Jews grew. In 1938, synagogues and Jewish-owned businesses were destroyed or damaged, and many male Jews were arrested and imprisoned at concentration camps. Other countries watched what was happening, but many did nothing to stop it. The Nazis saw they could get away with such cruelty and continued to increase their persecution against the Jews and others. In 1939, World War II began. Germany occupied many countries in Europe, and very quickly millions of Jews came under Nazi control. The Nazis began to place Jews into ghettos, separating them from their non-Jewish neighbors in isolated areas of various cities. But this short-term step to contain and control the Jews soon evolved into a plan that would lead to the mass murder of Jews across Europe.

*Top: The fortress at Terezin. **Left:** The slogan on the gate at Terezin means "Work sets you free." This Nazi slogan appeared on the gates of several concentration camps, including Auschwitz. **Center:** This classroom of children would later be deported to the ghetto. **Right:** Prisoners slept in the bunk beds in these barracks at Terezin.*

Left: *The tree at Terezin, 1946.* **Top center and top right:** *Monuments at Terezin remember those from the camp who died.* **Bottom right:** *A group of children at Terezin, 1945.*

In occupied Europe, millions of Jews were concentrated into various camps where life was very difficult. Many died. In 1941, the Nazis established a camp called Theresienstadt in German and Terezin by the people of Czechoslovakia. This camp-ghetto existed for three and a half years, from 1941 to 1945. It had four purposes. First, Theresienstadt served as a transit camp. From there, the Nazis deported the prisoners to death camps, concentration camps, and work camps. Second, Theresienstadt was a labor camp meant to maintain the myth that Jews were being deported to perform labor in "the east." Third, Theresienstadt was a "holding" camp, where the Nazis hoped poor conditions would cause prisoners to weaken and die while waiting to be transported to camps further east. Theresienstadt also served a propaganda purpose, falsely demonstrating the humane treatment of prisoners by the Nazis. In reality, conditions were horrifying—overcrowding, disease, hunger, and fear overwhelmed the ghetto-camp.

There were many rules. No one could walk on sidewalks. No one could sing or whistle. No one could pick flowers. People struggled each day to survive.

But within the darkness of Terezin, in this world of disorder, barbarity, and brutality, hope and life grew: the Children's Tree of Terezin.

Photographs of Irma Lauscher.

The Legacy of the Terezin Tree

Many people from Terezin died, at Terezin or when they were sent to other camps. Jiri and Irma Lauscher survived, as did their daughter Michaela. Michaela's correspondence was a valuable resource for this book.

What do you remember about arriving in Terezin?

I went to Terezin with my parents, our transport had 1,000 people, at first we went to the gathering barrack in Prague, from there altogether by train to Terezin and the last 2 km on foot. In one of the barracks in Terezin was the intake, families were separated, and we were ordered to our "accommodation"—men to men's barracks, etc., I came to a children's house.

Did you attend secret classes?

Yes, I attended secret classes. We were in this home, children aged from 5-9 years and learned together, the basic school subjects. Someone was always guarding. In the rest of the day we also had some programmes, but these things were no more illegal: e.g. played games, read books and drew and painted, listened to somebody's loud reading, reciting nursery rhymes, being taught to clean ourselves (mostly in cold water) and to keep our room tidy. We have to be very grateful to our tutors and teachers who tried to make our life as normal as possible in the hard conditions of the camp.

How did your mother get the sapling?

I do not know for sure, but my mother always said that someone brought it from outside the ghetto, inside his rubber boot.

TEREZIN CHILDREN'S TREE OF LIFE

GIFT FROM THE
JEWISH UNITED FUND/JEWISH FEDERATION
OF METROPOLITAN CHICAGO
MAY 6, 2009

ORIGINALLY PRESENTED
TO THE JUF PRIME MINISTER'S MISSION
IN HONOR OF
THEIR TRIP TO PRAGUE, CZECH REPUBLIC
IN NOVEMBER, 2004

A descendant of the original Terezin tree grows in Skokie, Illinos, at the Illinois Holocaust Museum and Education Center. It was gifted to the museum in 2009.

Over 600 sites around the world were given seeds and saplings from the original Terezin tree. The pictures on this page show the tree at the Illinois Holocaust Museum and Education Center in Skokie, Illinois. A partial list of places around the world that have grown trees from seeds and cuttings from the original tree from Terezin includes:

In the United States

Illinois Holocaust Museum and Education Center
Skokie, Illinois

Center for Holocaust and Humanity Education
Cincinnati, Ohio

United States Holocaust Memorial Museum
Washington, D.C.

Holocaust Museum and Learning Center
St. Louis, Missouri

Around the World

Beth Shalom Holocaust Centre
Surrey, United Kingdom

The National Holocaust Centre and Museum
Nottinghamshire, United Kingdom

Yad Vashem
Jerusalem, Israel

Terezin
Czech Republic

Saplings grow in the greenhouses at the Chicago Botanic Garden in Glencoe, Illinois. **Bottom left:** *Cathy Thomas, Director of the Woody Plants Division*

Saplings from the tree at the Illinois Holocaust Museum and Education Center in Skokie, Illinois, are being grown at the Chicago Botanic Garden. Many thanks to the Chicago Botanic Garden, and in particular Cathy Thomas, Director of the Woody Plants Division, who has taken care of the Terezin tree offspring in the Chicago Botanic Garden.

Dede Harris and her husband Sam

Author's Note

One day in May 2009, at the Illinois Holocaust Museum and Education Center (IHMEC), a group from the Chicago Jewish community witnessed the dedication of a small tree, descended from the legendary Terezin tree. My husband Sam and I were fortunate to be among this group. Sam is a child survivor of the Holocaust and President Emeritus of the IHMEC. I have been privileged to live in Sam's world, observing his efforts to educate children and adults through hundreds of speaking engagements. In addition to this unique vantage point, I am also a docent at IHMEC and a former schoolteacher.

During the Terezin tree dedication, I recognized the valuable life lessons to learn from the story of the Children's Tree of Terezin, not the least of which would be learning the painful story of the Holocaust itself. This poignant story captured my heart, and I vowed I would do something to carry it on. This idea would not go away. I trusted my small persistent voice telling me to keep the story of the Terezin tree alive. At the time, I had no idea I would write a book. I just knew when I heard the story, I had the responsibility to tell it to others. My first attempt was to capture the Terezin Tree Story in my Narrative Art Sculpture, Theresienstadt: From Terror to Transcendence. Slowly, my ideas crystallized, and with encouragement from my dear husband Sam, I committed not only to write this book, but to work with the Chicago Botanic Garden. Cuttings from our local Terezin Tree are currently nurtured and cared for by the Chicago Botanic Garden and will be sent out into the world, multiplying those who will learn about this story of the Children's Tree of Terezin. I shared my passion for this story with my dear friend Sara Akerlund, a dedicated docent at the IHMEC, who agreed to illustrate this book and shares my sense of responsibility to bring this story to as many as possible.

Acknowledgements

You might think that writing a book involves only one person, the writer. But that is not the case. A great many people were involved in giving birth to this book. Kelley Szany and Amanda Friedeman, educators from the Illinois Holocaust Museum and Education Center, reviewed this book, gave suggestions, and established a grade level. It was important to make sure this book was written at a level that would be comfortable for the reader.

My dear friend Ellen Palestrant has always encouraged my creative activities: the Holocaust trilogy, my art sculptures, and now *The Children's Tree of Terezin*. I trust Ellen's artistic judgment, that to share these stories that have touched my heart would touch others as well.

My special niece, Beth Kanter, added by graciously using her incredible skills editing.

Sara Akerlund worked with me every step of the way, generously offering ideas and her incredible creativity.

My wonderful family, Julie, Jeff, Jeremy and Jessica Kreamer, encouraged me, adding ideas and critiques.

And my dear husband Sam, very knowledgeable about history, offered useful information and ideas.

No wife, mother, aunt, or friend could ask for more support.

Resources

Without a doubt, our most valuable resources for this book were interviews with the actual child witnesses of Theresienstadt.

Lisl Bogart and Steen Metz, both on the speaker's bureau of the Illinois Holocaust Museum and Education Center, graciously and patiently contributed to this book by telling their personal stories about their young lives in Theresienstadt.

Other resources included the United States Holocaust Memorial Museum; the Center for Holocaust and Humanity Education in Cincinnati, Ohio; the Terezin Memorial Museum in the Czech Republic, and Yad Vashem.

Author's Bio

Dede Harris and her husband Sam live part-time in Kildeer, Illinois, and Scottsdale, Arizona. She graduated from the University of Illinois with a major in Elementary Education and the University of Chicago where she received her Master's Degree in Social Service Administration. Dede has worked as an elementary school teacher, social worker, insurance agent, and docent at the Illinois Holocaust Museum and Education Center. She is a wife, mother, grandmother, artist, and author.

Dede became interested in the Holocaust after her marriage to Sam, a child survivor of the Holocaust, and was instrumental in building the Illinois Holocaust Museum and Education Center. Because of her interest in the Holocaust, Dede created narrative, multimedia sculptures about life in three concentration camps: Ebensee, Auschwitz, and Theresienstadt. Each sculpture is accompanied by a booklet describing the meaning behind the materials used and the skills involved. A DVD, *A Holocaust Trilogy,* about these sculptures has been produced by Ellen Palestrant and Eric Cosh.

It is Dede's hope that all the readers of this true story, *The Children's Tree of Terezin,* will be inspired by the strength of Irma Lauscher and the children of Terezin.

Illustrator's Bio

Sara Akerlund was born in North Carolina and grew up in Minneapolis. She graduated from the University of Minnesota with a major in Elementary Education and a minor in science and history. After graduation, she taught first grade and loved the challenge of teaching science, history, and art to first graders intent on learning to read.

Sara has always had an avid interest in history. Her family history in America goes back to the 1700s and her grandparents helped cultivate her interest in learning about her family and the development of America.

As a teenager, she had many Jewish friends in Minneapolis and spent time with them learning about their traditions and history in Europe. She heard stories about their immigration to America and the family and friends they lost during the Holocaust. Because of these friendships, as an adult, Sara became interested in Jewish history, Jewish culture, and the Holocaust. She interviewed Holocaust survivors for the Shoah Foundation and has traveled to Poland and other Eastern European countries numerous times. She has visited Terezin twice and interviewed several survivors from that camp.

She is a docent at the IHMEC and enjoys painting for expression and enjoyment.

She lives in Caledonia, Illinois, with her husband Dan. They have three children and five grandchildren.

Glossary

Am Yisrael Chai—The People of Israel Live; title of a song sung in celebration

barrack—A building used to house large numbers of people

concentration camp—A place used by the Nazis to imprison people

contaminate—Make impure

Czechoslovakia—A country in central Europe that was occupied by the Germans during World War II. In 1993, Czechoslovakia was divided into two countries, with the western half becoming the Czech Republic and the eastern half becoming Slovakia.

dictator—A leader who has total power and rules by force

ghetto—An area set up to separate groups of people from the rest of the population

Hitler—Adolf Hitler was the leader of the National Democratic Socialist Worker's Party, known as the Nazi party

memorial—Something built to honor an event or a person

rabbi—A teacher

ration—A limited amount of food, water, or supplies. Because water was rationed in Terezin, each person was given a set amount they had to make last.

sapling—A young tree

selfless—Unselfish

slave labor—People forced to work without payment

testifying—Serving as proof of something's existence

transit—Moving from one place to another

Tu B'Shevat—A Jewish holiday celebrating the New Year for Trees

typhoid fever—A very contagious disease spread through food and water

visa—A legal paper issued by a government giving a citizen of one country permission to enter another country